HOW-TO SERIES

for the HR Professional

Building
Pay
Structures

Daniel P. Purushotham, Ph.D., CCP, CBP
Stephanie Y. Wilson, CCP

WorldatWork.

About WorldatWork*

WorldatWork is the world's leading not-for-profit professional association dedicated to knowledge leadership in compensation, benefits and total rewards. Founded in 1955, WorldatWork focuses on human resources disciplines associated with attracting, retaining and motivating employees. Besides serving as the membership association of the professions, the WorldatWork family of organizations provides education, certification (Certified Compensation Professional — CCP*, Certified Benefits Professional — CBP™ and Global Remuneration Professional — GRP*), publications, knowledge resources, surveys, conferences, research and networking. WorldatWork Society of Certified Professionals and Alliance for Work-Life Progress (AWLP) are part of the WorldatWork family.

The Professional Association for Compensation, Benefits and Total Rewards

WorldatWork
14040 N. Northsight Blvd., Scottsdale, AZ 85260
480/951-9191   Fax 480/483-8352
www.worldatwork.org

Publishing Manager: Dan Cafaro
Graphic Design: Mark Anthony Muñoz
Production Manager: Rebecca Williams Ficker
Staff Contributor: Andrea Ozias

Table of Contents

Chapter 4 — Pitfalls and Precautions 35

Introduction

C ompensation deals with establishing a meaningful and acceptable relationship between work and rewards. Work performed by employees should help organizations achieve their objectives. These objectives are derived from the organization's overall business strategy, which supports the company's mission statement.

When designed and administered appropriately, a company's compensation program is an effective management tool for supporting the organization's overall business strategy. A series of steps is used in the process of designing sound compensation programs. (See Figure 1 on page 7.) This process is not a one-time event. It involves constant review and refinement in light of changing business needs.

There are two broad categories of compensation: cash and noncash. The focus of this booklet is on cash compensation. Cash-compensation management has two distinct but interrelated aspects: content and process.

Content is managed through job analysis, evaluation and research to keep abreast of the changes in compensation levels in the external market.

Process includes tools and methods for collecting, calculating, organizing, storing and customizing internal and external information pertaining to compensation. The pay structure of an organization is one such tool. Within the context of cash-compensation management, process should support and not conflict with content.*

---

* Much of the information relating to content is addressed in other WorldatWork booklets: *Designing and Conducting a Salary Survey, Analyzing and Applying Salary Survey Information* and *Documenting Job Content.*

1

An Ideal
Compensation Program

M ost compensation professionals agree that the following "ideal" characteristics are necessary for every compensation program in order to attract, retain and motivate qualified employees. (Note: These characteristics are primarily for all positions except single incumbent senior management positions.) These characteristics are the foundation for an ideal pay structure:

- **Internal equity.** A measure of how an organization values each of its jobs in relation to one another.

- **External competitiveness.** A measure of an organization's pay structure compared to that of its competitors.

- **Affordability.** A measure of how costly a compensation program is to a company. If pay structures are not developed responsibly, an organization could incur labor costs that exceed what it can afford to pay.

- **Legally defensible.** Compensation programs must adhere to specific laws designed to provide fairness in how employees are paid. These laws include the Fair Labor Standards Act (FLSA), the Equal Pay Act, Title VII of the Civil Rights Act, the Age Discrimination in Employment Act and the Americans with Disabilities Act (ADA).

- **Understandable/saleable.** To be accepted and understood, compensation programs must be well communicated.*

- **Efficient to administer.** With increased pressure to improve productivity and reduce costs, it is important that an organization's compensation program be as simple and straightforward as possible to maintain and administer. A balance needs to be struck between what appears to be the "best" program and what is efficient, effective and easiest to administer.

- **Safeguard the organization's resources.** The compensation program should reward performance fairly without conflicting with the interests of company stakeholders. Rewards should reflect both individual employee and company performance. Human resources should be seen as an

* See also the WorldatWork booklet, *Communicating Compensation Programs.*

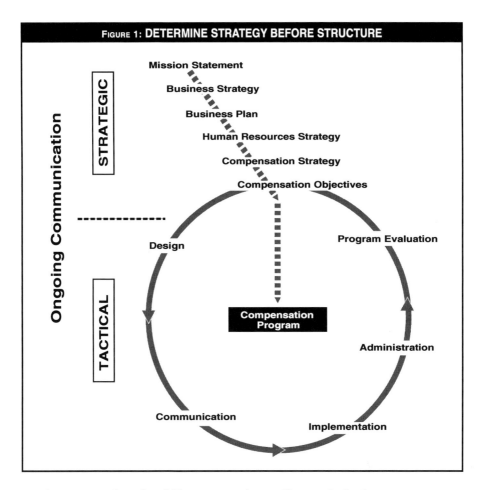

FIGURE 1: DETERMINE STRATEGY BEFORE STRUCTURE

STRATEGIC

Mission Statement
Business Strategy
Business Plan
Human Resources Strategy
Compensation Strategy
Compensation Objectives

Ongoing Communication

Design

Program Evaluation

TACTICAL

Compensation Program

Administration

Communication

Implementation

investment that should be protected as well as optimized.

- **Flexible.** Pay programs are tools necessary to compete for labor in the marketplace. As such, they must be flexible and capable of changing as needed, without having to be revamped every time a new need arises.

- **Meets the organization's unique needs.** To some degree, each company is unique within its own industry or geographical area. Unique characteristics need to be recognized and addressed when designing compensation programs and, particularly, pay structures.

Most compensation programs, however, will not include all these characteristics. In fact, some of these characteristics may be in conflict with each other. For example, it may not always be possible to maintain internal equity when a company is trying to be externally competitive. Therefore, it is important to recognize the possibility of such conflict and to review the business strategy to determine the appropriate balance of all features of the compensation program.

Pay Structures

A pay structure consists of a series of pay ranges, or "grades," each with a minimum and maximum pay rate. Jobs are grouped together in ranges that represent similar internal and external worth. (See Figure 2.)

The midpoint or middle-pay value for the range usually represents the competitive market value for a job or group of jobs. The company's base-pay policy line connects the midpoints of the various pay ranges in the pay structure.

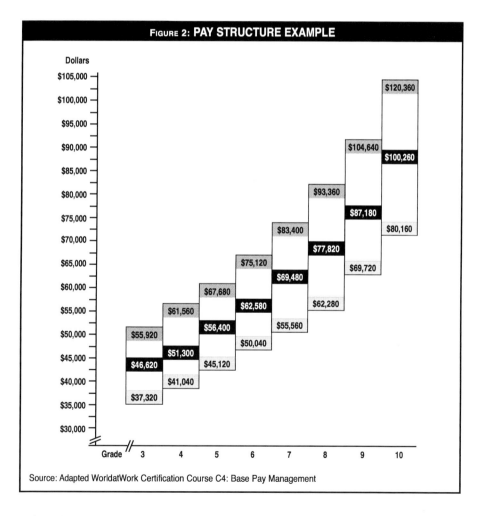

FIGURE 2: **PAY STRUCTURE EXAMPLE**

Source: Adapted WorldatWork Certification Course C4: Base Pay Management

In recent years, pay policy lines have been developed to reflect base salary midpoints and also to take into consideration variable compensation. For the purpose of this discussion, the design and development of pay structures will be confined to base salary, representing all positions except single incumbent senior management positions.

General and Specific Factors Affecting Pay Structures

Pay structures are influenced by the following *general* factors:

- **Corporate culture and values.** An organization's pay structure usually reflects the way employees' work is valued. For example, does an organization always look for the best and brightest employees? If so, the pay line may be positioned to lead the market. If the organization encourages and values prudent risk-taking, the total pay line may have an additional risk/reward component.

- **Management philosophy.** Narrow pay ranges and more grades allow for more frequent promotions — and a greater perception of "growth and advancement" — than wider ranges and fewer grades. However, if management believes in promoting employees only when duties and responsibilities change significantly, the distances between midpoints of ranges may be as substantial as 15 percent or more.

- **External economic environment.** Varied supply and demand for certain skills may necessitate a multistructured pay program. Technical professionals such as engineers may have special pay structures when there is a high demand for their skills. However, these special structures may be merged into the general structure when there is an increase in the supply of engineers in the market. Other external factors that may be reflected in pay structures include inflationary fluctuations and cost-of-living indices such as the Consumer Price Index (CPI).

- **External socio-political and legal environments.** The "steps" in the pay structure are likely to be more narrow and rigidly administered in a union environment than in a nonunion environment. Pay structures also are affected by regulations such as the FLSA, which mandates the minimum wage for most jobs and thereby determines the lowest possible pay scale.

Several other factors that influence pay structures relate directly to the operations and culture of a *specific* organization:

- **Centralized compensation policy.** A corporate compensation policy may call for the organization's overall competitive posture to always be ahead of the market. This will be reflected in the pay policy line being higher than the market at every point on the salary range. On the other hand, the strategy could be to hire employees at a rate always higher than the market but over time to bring them in line with the market. This would mean steadily fine-tuning the pay ranges at different levels.

- **Decentralized compensation policy.** An organization's goal may be to compete within the top quartile of its competitors in a particular functional segment (e.g., sales/marketing) or product segment (e.g., jet engines or disability income insurance). In this case, the pay structure may be different for those particular functional and product segments within the organization.

- **Short-term vs. long-term orientation.** A company with long-term orientation is most likely to have well-designed pay structures with career-path capabilities and smooth transitions from range to range. The ranges themselves will be developed after much thought and research. Short-term or temporary problems need to be taken care of with temporary solutions. **Solving temporary problems with long-term solutions should be avoided.** Employees generally have an entitlement mind-set with respect to compensation, and it may be difficult to "undo" prior actions, even though the original reasons for such actions no longer exist.

2

Anatomy of a Pay Structure

A pay structure has multiple pay or salary ranges. Every pay structure has key components that are critical to its overall design. The following section defines and describes these basic elements.

Pay Ranges and Range Spreads

A "pay range" has a minimum pay value, a maximum pay value and a "midpoint" or central value. The difference between the maximum and the minimum is the "range spread," or the "width" of the range. Range width usually is expressed as a percentage of the difference between the minimum and maximum divided by the minimum. For example, in Figure 3 on page 13, the range spread in dollars for Grade 10 (from Figure 2), where the maximum is $120,360 and the minimum is $80,160, is $120,360 – $80,160 = $40,200. The percentage is about 50 percent, or $40,200 divided by $80,160.

To calculate the spread on either side of the midpoint, use the formulas shown in the box below (where $100,260 is the Grade 10 midpoint in Figure 2).

A pay range with a 50-percent range spread will have a 20-percent spread on either side of the midpoint. (See Figure 3.) That is, $80,160 is 80 percent of $100,260, and $120,360 is 120 percent of $100,260.

While all the ranges in Figure 2 have a range spread of 50 percent, the spread does not have to be uniform throughout the pay structure. Figure 4 on page 14 lists common range spreads and their corresponding spreads on either side of the midpoint.

Example 1 on page 13 shows how to calculate the spread on either side of the midpoint. To perform the calculation, one of the three points (minimum, midpoint or maximum) on the pay range needs to be specified along with the range width.

CALCULATION OF SPREAD ON EITHER SIDE OF MIDPOINT

$$\frac{\text{Midpoint - Minimum}}{\text{Midpoint}} = \frac{\$100{,}260 - \$80{,}160}{\$100{,}260} = -20\% \text{ of Midpoint}$$

$$\frac{\text{Maximum - Midpoint}}{\text{Midpoint}} = \frac{\$120{,}360 - \$100{,}260}{\$100{,}260} = +20\% \text{ of Midpoint}$$

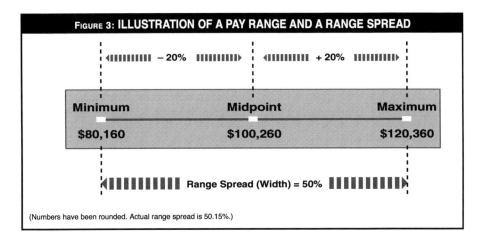

Figure 3: ILLUSTRATION OF A PAY RANGE AND A RANGE SPREAD

– 20%   + 20%

Minimum	Midpoint	Maximum
$80,160	$100,260	$120,360

Range Spread (Width) = 50%

(Numbers have been rounded. Actual range spread is 50.15%.)

Using a range spread of about 50 percent and a minimum of $80,160, the maximum and midpoint are calculated as in Example 1.

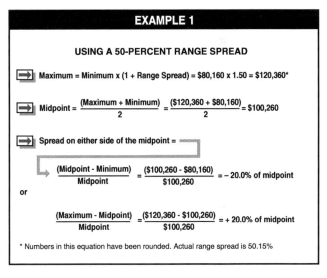

EXAMPLE 1

USING A 50-PERCENT RANGE SPREAD

➡ Maximum = Minimum x (1 + Range Spread) = $80,160 x 1.50 = $120,360*

➡ Midpoint = $\frac{(Maximum + Minimum)}{2}$ = $\frac{($120,360 + $80,160)}{2}$ = $100,260

➡ Spread on either side of the midpoint =

$\frac{(Midpoint - Minimum)}{Midpoint}$ = $\frac{($100,260 - $80,160)}{$100,260}$ = – 20.0% of midpoint

or

$\frac{(Maximum - Midpoint)}{Midpoint}$ = $\frac{($120,360 - $100,260)}{$100,260}$ = + 20.0% of midpoint

* Numbers in this equation have been rounded. Actual range spread is 50.15%

Some Practical Considerations

Range spreads vary based on the level and sophistication of skills required for a given position. Entry-level positions that require skills that are quickly mastered usually have narrower pay ranges than supervisory, managerial or higher-level technical positions. Individuals in lower-level positions not only master the requirements of the job sooner, they also have a greater number of opportunities over time to be promoted to higher-level positions. Senior-level positions require a longer learning curve and often have limited opportunities for advancement. The following are typical range spreads for different kinds of positions:

- 20 percent-25 percent: lower-level service, production and maintenance
- 30 percent-40 percent: clerical, technical, paraprofessional

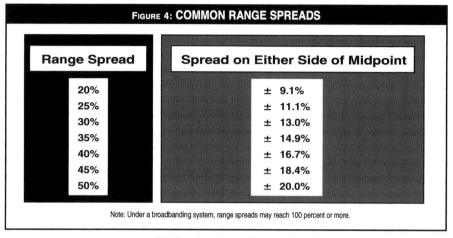

Figure 4: COMMON RANGE SPREADS

Range Spread	Spread on Either Side of Midpoint
20%	± 9.1%
25%	± 11.1%
30%	± 13.0%
35%	± 14.9%
40%	± 16.7%
45%	± 18.4%
50%	± 20.0%

Note: Under a broadbanding system, range spreads may reach 100 percent or more.

- 40 percent-50 percent: higher-level professional, administrative, middle management

- 50 percent and above: higher-level managerial, executive, technical

Care should be taken when deciding pay-range width. Assuming a constant midpoint, changing range spreads also changes the minimum and maximum. Notice in Example 2 below that as the ranges get wider, the maximums increase, the minimums decrease and the midpoints are constant.

Ranges should be designed to provide midpoints that reflect the "going rate" and are reasonably close to what the market establishes as the minimum and maximum for the job. Minimums that are too low

EXAMPLE 2

Range Spread	Minimum	Midpoint	Maximum
30%	$27,826	$32,000	$36,174
40%	$26,667	$32,000	$37,333
50%	$25,600	$32,000	$38,400

will result in a company needing to pay an employee higher in the range in order to pay competitively. This narrows the position's long-term earning potential. In turn, a high maximum may provide long-term earnings opportunities that are higher and more costly than what are needed to be competitive.

Midpoints

The midpoint is a key element in pay administration. It is often used as a reference point in salary administration decisions as a point or "target." The midpoint is usually the reference used because it is typically set to equal the market average or median. It should not be an organization's only market reference point.

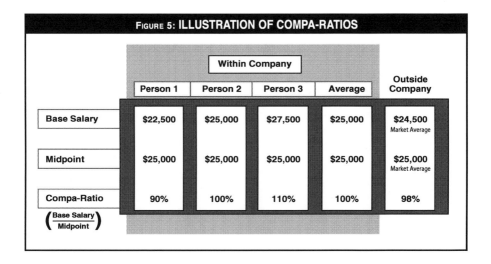

FIGURE 5: ILLUSTRATION OF COMPA-RATIOS

	Within Company				Outside Company
	Person 1	Person 2	Person 3	Average	
Base Salary	$22,500	$25,000	$27,500	$25,000	$24,500 Market Average
Midpoint	$25,000	$25,000	$25,000	$25,000	$25,000 Market Average
Compa-Ratio $\left(\dfrac{\text{Base Salary}}{\text{Midpoint}}\right)$	90%	100%	110%	100%	98%

Related to the midpoint is the compa-ratio, a statistic that expresses the relationship between base salary and the midpoint, or between the midpoint and market average. Figure 5 illustrates the calculation of compa-ratio for the same job as well as for the market average. Compa-ratios can be calculated for individuals, groups of individuals and the company as a whole.

Most companies strive to have the overall workforce paid at or around a compa-ratio of 100 percent. Individual compa-ratios vary according to how long the individual has been in the job, previous work experience and job performance. A mature, long-service work force will tend to have a higher compa-ratio (often above 100 percent) than a younger group of employees with a shorter service record.

It is important for a company to be able to explain the reasons for its current compa-ratio. Businesses monitor compa-ratios because they recognize them as an important tool for managing compensation costs. In some cases, companies cap pay at the midpoint for the purpose of paying "at market" for base salaries. The remainder of the range is available only to high performers and often is paid on a lump-sum basis from year to year. These companies increase base salaries only when range midpoints move and their compa-ratios drop below 100 percent.

Range Penetration
Another way of tracking an organization's compensation is to view employee pay in relationship to the total pay range. This is known as range penetration.

Unlike compa-ratios, which are calculated using a grade's midpoint, range penetration is calculated using the minimum and maximum of a salary

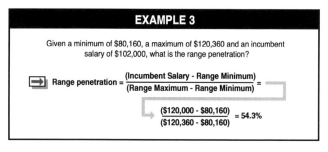

range. Range penetration is shown above in Example 3.

Often range penetration is a preferred tool because it does not focus on one number alone, the midpoint. Instead, it refers to how far into the range a particular individual's salary has penetrated. Range profiles often are used in conjunction with either the compa-ratio or range penetration to describe where employees should expect their pay to fall in relationship to their pay range over time. (See Figure 6.)

Midpoint Progression

Midpoint progression refers to the percentage difference between pay-grade midpoints. The larger the midpoint progression, the fewer the number of

FIGURE 6: ILLUSTRATION OF RANGE PENETRATION

Year	Minimum	Midpoint	Maximum	Salary	Range Penetration
1	$15,360	$19,200	$23,040	$15,360	0.00%
2	$15,744	$19,680	$23,616	$16,282	6.83%
3	$16,138	$20,172	$24,206	$17,260	13.90%
4	$16,541	$20,676	$24,811	$18,294	21.19%
5	$16,955	$21,193	$25,432	$19,393	28.76%
6	$17,382	$21,724	$26,068	$20,555	36.56%
7	$17,813	$22,266	$26,719	$21,788	44.64%
8	$18,258	$22,823	$27,388	$23,095	52.99%
9	$18,715	$23,393	$28,072	$24,481	61.62%
10	$19,182	$23,978	$28,774	$25,950	70.56%
11	$19,662	$24,577	$29,494	$27,508	79.80%
12	$20,154	$25,192	$30,230	$29,159	89.36%
13	$20,658	$25,822	$30,986	$30,907	99.24%

$$\text{Range penetration} = \frac{(\text{Salary} - \text{Minimum})}{(\text{Maximum} - \text{Minimum})}$$

Constant Range Width: 50%

Constant Annual Range Movement (Structure Change): 2.5%

Constant Salary Increase: 4%

Given the above constants and a starting salary of $12,800, it would take:

- **8 years** to exceed the **midpoint** ($22,823) of the range
- **13 years** to reach close to the **maximum** ($30,986) of the range

By changing any one of the three constants, the extent of range penetration could be increased or decreased. The actual progression in the range is determined by the difference between range movement and the amount of salary increase.

grades within a pay structure. Conversely, the smaller the midpoint progression, the larger the number of pay grades within the pay structure.

Three Approaches to Developing Midpoints

One approach to developing midpoints is the present value — future value formula, which may be used to determine the percentage between midpoints, assuming the highest and lowest midpoints and the number of grades are known. The formula shown in the box below may be used, or the calculations may be performed on a business calculator.

Suppose a company wishes to develop a pay structure with six grades that has a highest midpoint of $77,820 and a lowest midpoint of $46,620. What is the midpoint progression?

Using the formula below, the midpoint progression is calculated to be 12.5 percent. The resulting pay structure looks like Figure 7.

There are two other approaches to developing midpoints and the resulting midpoint progression. The first is to use the average of the market pay rate for different jobs within benchmark-

PRESENT VALUE — FUTURE VALUE FORMULA

$$PV = \frac{FV}{(1 + i)^n}$$

	DEFINITION	VALUE
PV	Present value (midpoint of lowest pay grade)	$46,620
FV	Future value (midpoint of the highest pay grade)	$77,820
n	Number of desired grade intervals (one less than the total number of grades in the structure)	4
i	Percentage difference between midpoints	To be determined

Using these values, i = 12.5%

FIGURE 7: EXAMPLE OF MIDPOINT PROGRESSION

Grade	Midpoint	Midpoint Progression
3	$46,620	12.5%
4	$51,300	12.5%
5	$56,400	12.5%
6	$62,580	12.5%
7	$69,480	12.5%
8	$77,820	12.5%

(Numbers have been rounded.)

job groupings. The resulting midpoint progression would have varying percentage differences between midpoints, which reflect the market more closely than constant differences. An organization's pay structure need not have a constant percentage progression — it may remain uneven without being smoothed. In such instances, it should be recognized that promotional increases may be uneven and sometimes difficult to administer because of the following reasons:

- If the percentage difference between midpoints is too high, the result could be costly promotional increases.

- If the percentage difference is relatively low, the result could be salary compression problems between supervisory and subordinate positions and difficulty in matching promotions with appropriate compensatory rewards.

The other approach to develop midpoints in a pay structure is the use of regression analysis. The advantage of this approach is it helps align market rates more closely with company policy. Regression analysis works well when job-evaluation points are used to develop pay structures. With the advent of more sophisticated technology, much of the statistical work can be done with the use of computers or powerful calculators.*

Exercising salary judgments within a segment often is easier and more practical than focusing rigidly on a single point within the salary range, such as the midpoint.

Pay Grades

The purpose of grades is to be able to refer to a compensation range that groups together multiple jobs with similar value based on internal comparisons and external market data. Grades need not always be numerical; alpha grades can serve the purpose just as well. Pay grades can be established by a number of methods.

* See also the WorldatWork booklet, *Mastering Market Data*.

There are many grades or levels within a pay structure. The number of grades used by a particular organization will vary based on findings from market research as well as the company's compensation policy. Does the policy call for frequent "promotions," or does it allow for real promotions when the major functions in the new job are of a higher value to the employees? Does the company want a "flat" organization, or does it prefer multiple levels within the organization?

Segmentation of Pay Grades

A pay grade may be segmented or subdivided in many ways — thirds, quartiles, quintiles and so on. These segments may or may not overlap. They serve as reference points for cost control and pay administration. The number of segments within a pay grade varies by company, and it often reflects the company's merit pay process and pay administration philosophy.

Using segments within a pay grade instead of only midpoints provides more flexibility to managers in pay-related decisions. These segments serve as mini-ranges within the main range. Exercising salary judgments within a segment often is easier and more practical than focusing rigidly on a single point within the salary range, such as the midpoint.

Pay-Grade Overlap

Pay grades usually overlap. Except for the minimum of the lowest grade and the maximum of the highest grade, minimums and maximums usually fall within adjoining ranges. The width of the pay grade and the midpoint differentials determine the amount of overlap between adjoining grades. Grade overlap is minimal when midpoint differentials are large and range widths are small. (See Figure 8A on page 20.) Grade overlap is significant when midpoint differentials are small and range spread is large. (See Figure 8B on page 20.) Figures 8C on page 20 and 8D on page 21 are illustrations of moderate grade overlap.

In a pay-for-performance or merit system, grade overlap allows high performers in lower pay ranges with longer time-in-grade to be paid more than a relatively new (and/or lower) performer in a higher pay range. However, overlapping more than three or four pay grades generally should be avoided. Too much overlap limits the difference between midpoints, which in turn places limits on potential earning ability and can cause differentiation problems between supervisor and subordinate pay.

Multiple Pay Structures

An organization may have many pay structures within its overall structure. The number of structures is primarily a function of the market and the company's compensation philosophy. For instance, the ranges for certain professionals such as information systems and technology and investment management may call for a separate structure that cannot be force-fit into a typical "corporate" structure.

Different labor markets with different levels of supply and demand may necessitate multiple pay structures. Such pay structures allow greater flexibility in pay administration. Different groupings of positions such as clerical, blue collar jobs versus technical and professional

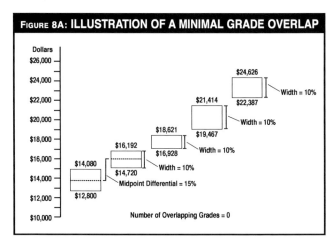

FIGURE 8A: **ILLUSTRATION OF A MINIMAL GRADE OVERLAP**

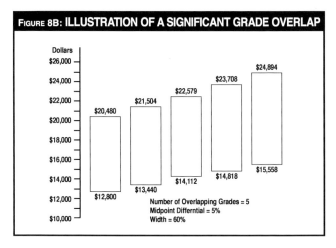

FIGURE 8B: **ILLUSTRATION OF A SIGNIFICANT GRADE OVERLAP**

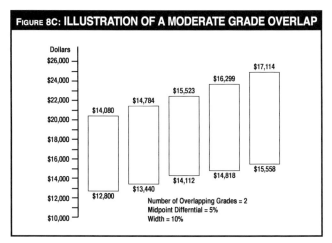

FIGURE 8C: **ILLUSTRATION OF A MODERATE GRADE OVERLAP**

jobs usually reflect different labor markets depending on supply and demand. Therefore, the slope of the pay lines could be different for different job families.

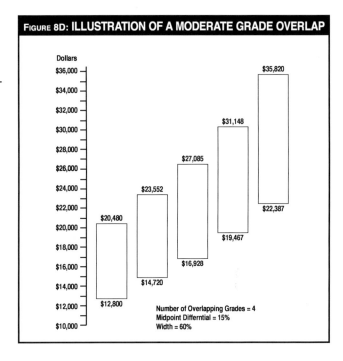

FIGURE 8D: ILLUSTRATION OF A MODERATE GRADE OVERLAP

Dollars

Number of Overlapping Grades = 4
Midpoint Differntial = 15%
Width = 60%

·

3

Developing a Pay Structure

T here are two basic considerations to factor into the design and development of pay structures: internal equity and external competitiveness.

Internal Equity

Internal equity refers to the relative values assigned to different jobs within an organization and how reasonable those values are, both within job families and among comparable jobs throughout the organization. Internal equity can be examined horizontally and vertically, as shown in Figure 9 on page 25. In this example, Departments A and B demonstrate horizontal internal equity in all three jobs because the salaries are fairly close. These departments also demonstrate vertical internal equity because there is a similar progression within the job hierarchy. Department C, however, demonstrates neither horizontal nor vertical internal equity.

Although horizontal and vertical internal equity are presented as two separate concepts, in reality they are interrelated. While it is appropriate to pay the Secretary Level III more than Levels I and II, how much more is determined by what is being done in the other two departments. (There are other factors that also must be factored in, such as performance and time-in-grade.)

The purpose of this illustration is to emphasize the importance of equity in salary administration and also to point out the different perspectives from which equity needs to be viewed. Internal equity is a key consideration in developing pay structures not only within a job family, as shown in the illustration of secretarial positions, but also among various job families that have common job grades. The first step in establishing internal equity is job evaluation.*

---

* See also the WorldatWork booklet, *Evaluating Job Content.*

		◀▪▪▪▪▪▪▪▪▪▪▪ Horizontal ▪▪▪▪▪▪▪▪▪▪▪▶		
		(Across departments or organizational units)		
▲▪▪▪ Vertical ▪▪▪▪ (Within departments or organizational units)	**Position**	**Department A**	**Department B**	**Department C**
		Salary	**Salary**	**Salary**
	Secretary Level I	$25,000	$26,000	$29,000
	Secretary Level II	$30,000	$31,000	$25,000
	Secretary Level III	$35,000	$36,000	$50,000

External Competitiveness

The other basic consideration in the design and development of pay structures is external competitiveness, or external equity. Businesses compete in a free market for products and services. The costs of these products and services include labor, which is never constant. Companies need to closely monitor labor costs to make sure that they neither overpay (leading to a higher cost than necessary in providing a product or service) nor underpay (possibly leading to higher turnover, which could hurt productivity).

The labor market is subject to the same external pressures as the product and services market. Organizations have to respond quickly, appropriately and consistently to survive constant changes in the labor market. It is important that the company's pay structure be capable of accommodating such changes.

Defining Competition

In researching a company's competitive posture, the first step is the definition of "competition." During times of low turnover, it may be more difficult to identify organizations that compete for labor. Low turnover should not lead to the false conclusion that there are no competitors for labor or that the compensation program is working perfectly for a given organization.

Turnover statistics may show which skills are in demand — and, in turn, which special pay structures may be necessary. However, turnover statistics by themselves may not reveal much about competitiveness. Terminations may be taking place for many reasons, both personal and professional. If employees are leaving particular companies for reasons other than increased pay — for example, to start their own businesses — these companies should be excluded from the defined list of competitors.

Once it is established that employees are moving to other companies, it is time to gather data on these businesses. In the final analysis, a company's human resources strategic plan must tie directly to the data gathered on any defined competition. In general, companies tend to survey other businesses similar to themselves in all or some of the following characteristics: size (usually reflected by total assets), industry type (products, services), geographical location, revenue/income size and required job skills. Here are three ways to obtain data:

- Refer to published surveys. Before using published surveys, carefully review their usefulness and applicability to the organization. It may be possible to examine the survey input documents as well as an extract of survey output.

- Participate in customized surveys. When possible, participate in customized surveys conducted by other companies of similar size or industry type.

- Conduct a survey. If data are required in a hurry, a telephone survey may be conducted. However, telephone surveys are not recommended for multiple jobs because the amount of phone time required may not be convenient for all participants.

Before a company decides to conduct its own survey, there are obvious considerations such as time, costs, usefulness of data and survey purpose. There also are some hidden concerns, such as the difficulty of convincing potential peer organizations to participate.*

Key Steps in Designing an Effective Pay Structure

The following set of steps describes the specific ways in which internal equity and external competitiveness both play a role in establishing pay structures and job hierarchy. (See Figure 10 on page 27.) These steps are based on the assumption that the organization is using a point-factor job-evaluation plan, one of the many methods of establishing the value of a job internally.

After the description of each step, key issues pertaining to that step are highlighted and questions to be asked regarding each issue are indicated. Specific answers to these questions are not given because they would differ from organization to organization.

Note that the first five steps relate to the establishment of internal equity. The last five steps relate to external competitiveness. In general, as the job

---

* See also the WorldatWork booklet, *Measuring the Marketplace*.

FIGURE 10: INTERNAL EQUITY EXAMPLE

FIGURE 10: INTERNAL EQUITY EXAMPLE

Internal Equity	External Competitiveness
■ Review overall point differentials	■ Incorporate market data
■ Rank order jobs by total evaluation points	■ Review market inconsistencies
■ Develop job groupings	■ Smooth out grade averages
■ Develop preliminary point bands	■ Review differences between midpoints and market averages
■ Check intrafamily and supervisory relationships	■ Resolve inconsistencies between internal and external equity

level increases, the reliance on external market data — as opposed to internal considerations — also increases. (See Figure 11 on page 29.)

Step 1: Review Overall Point Differentials

This step is often referred to as "sore thumbing" because it involves reviewing all of the job-evaluation points to see if any evaluations stand out from the group. If necessary, points are changed to better reflect the internal value of the job before proceeding to the second step.

Key issue: Do any job evaluations appear to be "out of place," either with their peers across functions or with their superiors or subordinates?

Key questions to ask: Do the evaluators fully understand the jobs? Is the job description or questionnaire complete? Is the job being compared to the correct peer group? Is the rater evaluating the job or the person?

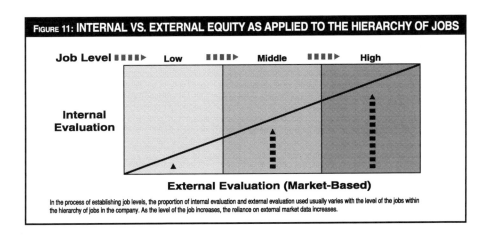

FIGURE 11: INTERNAL VS. EXTERNAL EQUITY AS APPLIED TO THE HIERARCHY OF JOBS

In the process of establishing job levels, the proportion of internal evaluation and external evaluation used usually varies with the level of the jobs within the hierarchy of jobs in the company. As the level of the job increases, the reliance on external market data increases.

Step 2: Rank Order Jobs by Total Evaluation Points

Rank all jobs in ascending or descending order as shown in Example 4.

Key issue: Does the hierarchy of positions make intuitive sense?

Key questions to ask: Does the hierarchy reflect the differences in the functions of the various positions? Has any position been overrated or underrated? Do the differences in points reflect the degree of differences between positions?

Step 3: Develop Job Groupings

While developing groupings, look for point breaks. Make sure that the number of levels identified is compatible with the number of levels within the organization. Possible job groupings using natural point breaks are shown in Example 5.

Key issue: How to develop job groupings that are meaningful rather than contrived.

Key questions to ask: Where are the natural point breaks? How many levels should there be to accommodate levels within the organization?

Step 4: Develop Preliminary Point Bands

Salary-grade point bands, or ranges, can be developed as either "absolute" point spreads or as percentage-based

EXAMPLE 4		
Rank Order	Job Title	Points
13	Claims Officer	565
12	Accounting Systems Control Officer	550
11	Employee Relations Officer	545
10	Team Leader	470
9	Senior Accounting Consultant	425
8	Project Coordinator	405
7	Accounting Technician	355
6	Accounting Consultant	355
5	Records Management Specialist	345
4	Reconciliation Technician	335
3	Service Center Coordinator	260
2	Copy Center Worker	210
1	Mail Clerk	140

EXAMPLE 5	
Job Groupings	
Claims Officer	565
Accounting Systems Control Officer	550
Employee Relations Officer	545
Team Leader	470
Senior Accounting Consultant	425
Project Coordinator	405
Accounting Technician	355
Accounting Consultant	355
Records Management Specialist	345
Reconciliation Technician	335
Service Center Coordinator	260
Copy Center Worker	210
Mail Clerk	140

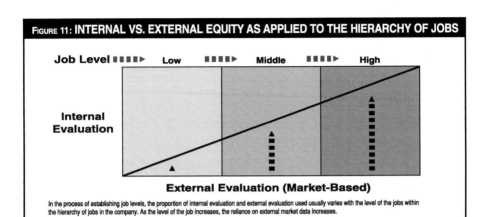

Figure 11: INTERNAL VS. EXTERNAL EQUITY AS APPLIED TO THE HIERARCHY OF JOBS

Job Level ▪▪▪▪▶   Low   ▪▪▪▪▶   Middle   ▪▪▪▪▶   High

Internal Evaluation

External Evaluation (Market-Based)

In the process of establishing job levels, the proportion of internal evaluation and external evaluation used usually varies with the level of the jobs within the hierarchy of jobs in the company. As the level of the job increases, the reliance on external market data increases.

point spreads be-tween point-band maximums. Table 1 is an example of an absolute point spread based on some of the jobs in the preceding examples. Notice that 39 points is the absolute value between point-band maximums. However, the percentage spread varies.

A variation on the "absolute" point spread is to increase the point spread when moving up the salary-grade structure. Companies may choose to do this in recognition of the broader range of skills represented

TABLE 1

GRADE	POINT BANDS		CONSTANT ABSOLUTE POINTS	VARYING PERCENTAGE SPREAD (rounded)
	MINIMUM	MAXIMUM		
1	137	178		
			39	22%
2	176	217		
			39	18%
3	215	256		
			39	15%
4	254	295		
			39	13%
5	293	334		
			39	12%
6	332	373		

TABLE 2

GRADE	POINT BANDS		VARYING ABSOLUTE POINTS	VARYING PERCENTAGE SPREAD (rounded)
	MINIMUM	MAXIMUM		
1	140	165		
			15	9%
2	166	180		
			35	19%
3	181	215		
			35	16%
4	216	250		
			40	16%
5	251	290		
			40	14%
6	291	330		

TABLE 3

GRADE	POINT BANDS		VARYING ABSOLUTE POINTS	CONSTANT PERCENTAGE SPREAD (rounded)
	MINIMUM	MAXIMUM		
1	126	145		
			22	15%
2	146	167		
			25	15%
3	168	192		
			29	15%
4	193	221		
			33	15%
5	222	254		
			38	15%
6	255	292		

within higher salary grades. Table 2 on page 29 is an example.

An alternate approach is to develop point bands with percentage-based point spreads

TABLE 4

GRADE	POINT BANDS		VARYING ABSOLUTE POINTS	VARYING PERCENTAGE SPREAD (rounded)
	MINIMUM	MAXIMUM		
1	126	145		
2	146	167	22	15%
3	169	192	25	15%
4	199	225	33	17%
5	230	263	38	17%
6	275	313	50	19%

between point-band maximums. The percentage spread can remain constant or vary. Tables 3 and 4 on page 29 are examples.

Key issue: Determining the width of each point band.

Key questions to ask: Wider point bands will require fewer grades, and they will group a larger number of jobs together. Is this in line with company's corporate policy? Are jobs with similar skill, effort and responsibility being grouped together?

For the purposes of this example, a salary structure will be constructed with 11 grades. It is important to remember that this decision is not purely objective. It takes into account an organization's internal values and other practical considerations such as the desired number of grades or a set policy regarding the number of grades between supervisor and employee. Most importantly, the structure should work for the company.

The point bands in Example 6 were developed using job evaluations and the natural breaks between jobs. A minimum of 137 points was set for the lowest grade, which is occupied by the Mail Clerk job (evaluated at 140 points). Each grade's point-band width is a constant 39 points between point-band maximums. The 11 grades, shown in Example 6, are designed to accommodate the lowest-level job — Mail Clerk — to the highest-level job — Claims Officer.

EXAMPLE 6

Grade	Point Bands
11	527 +
10	488-526
9	449-487
8	410-448
7	371-409
6	332-370
5	293-331
4	254-292
3	215-253
2	176-214
1	137-175

Step 5: Check Intrafamily and Supervisory Relationships

The last step in the internal equity process is to check the evaluations to ensure they represent all the levels and reporting relationships within the organization. It is important to determine whether jobs of similar skill, effort, responsibility and working conditions are within the same salary level. The structure should be reviewed to ensure that dissimilar jobs are not placed within the same level, and that subordinate and supervisor positions are not placed within the same grade.

Key issue: Peer and subordinate/superior relationships.

Key questions to ask: Are there enough levels between supervisor and subordinate positions? Do the set levels accurately reflect levels within job families?

Step 6: Incorporate Market Data

Based on the preliminary ranking performed in Steps 4 and 5, market data are added to identify differences in how your company and the market value a particular set of jobs.

Table 5 is an example.

Key issue: How to obtain the best fit between internal evaluation and market value.

TABLE 5

GRADE	POSITION	MARKET AVERAGE
11	Claims Officer Accounting Systems Control Officer Employee Relations Officer	$57,000 $53,000 $49,000
10	Open	
9	Team Leader	$36,000
8	Senior Accounting Consultant	$31,600
7	Project Coordinator	$29,200
6	Accounting Technician Accounting Consultant Records Management Specialist	$25,600 $24,300 $23,000
5	Reconciliation Technician	$23,000
4	Service Center Coordinator	$20,300
3	Open	
2	Copy Center Worker	$18,000
1	Mail Clerk	$15,300

Key questions to ask: Are the market numbers reliable? Are the job matches appropriate? How many open grades are needed to meet future needs? Is it possible to keep the market comparisons current?

At this point in the process, differences between a company's internal values for a job and the market's values become apparent. In Example 7 on page 32, note that there is only a 20-point difference between the evaluations for the Employee Relations Officer and the Claims Officer but an $8,000 difference in pay.

Step 7: Review Market Inconsistencies

At this point, the organization must decide the importance of the internal values that have been placed on its positions. It also must decide whether it can afford to pay differently than the market. Can the organization risk the internal integrity of the compensation program by relying more heavily on the market value of these positions? Are there enough positions within a job family to justify establishing a separate salary structure to address these problems?

EXAMPLE 7		
Job Title (Grade)	Points	Market Average
Claims Officer (11)	565	$57,000
Accounting Systems Control Officer (11)	550	$53,000
Employee Relations Officer (11)	545	$49,000
Open (10)		
Team Leader (9)	470	$36,000
Senior Accounting Consultant (8)	425	$31,600
Project Coordinator (7)	405	$29,200
Accounting Technician (6)	355	$25,600
Accounting Consultant (6)	355	$24,300
Records Management Specialist (6)	345	$23,000
Reconciliation Technician (5)	335	$23,000
Service Center Coordinator (4)	260	$20,300
Open (3)		
Copy Center Worker (2)	210	$18,000
Mail Clerk (1)	140	$15,300

Once any inconsistencies between the internal and external markets have been resolved, "raw" averages for jobs in each of the salary grades are calculated. These averages are simple means calculated from the market data. (See Table 6.)

Key issue: The company must decide whether it can accept a salary structure with varying percentages between its midpoints.

Key questions to ask: Is the number of grades selected (11) still acceptable? Can

TABLE 6		
GRADE	RAW MARKET AVERAGE	% DIFFERENCE
11	$53,000	
10	Open	
9	$36,000	
8	$31,600	13.9%
7	$29,200	8.2%
6	$24,300	20.2%
5	$23,000	5.7%
4	$20,300	13.3%
3	Open	
2	$18,000	
1	$15,300	17.6%

the differences between midpoints be smoothed
out without affecting the integrity of the market
competitiveness? How important is it to be close
to the market?

Step 8: Smooth Out Grade Averages

While smoothing out grade averages, a decision
has to be made on where it is most important to
be competitive and where the most payroll dollars
are at stake. Then test to see which midpoint-to-
midpoint percentage increment is the most logical
to use.

Example 8 has made use of 13.229-percent
increments, which allow for use of the 11 grades
proposed earlier. (These increments may be
derived using the "present value" formula discussed on page 17.)

EXAMPLE 8	
Grade	Proposed Midpoints
11	$53,000
10	$46,807
9	$41,338
8	$36,509
7	$32,243
6	$28,476
5	$25,149
4	$22,211
3	$19,616
2	$17,324
1	$15,300

Key issue: The company must decide whether there is an "ideal" midpoint-
to-midpoint percentage spread.

Key questions to ask: Is smoothing out always necessary or desirable?
Because the smoothing-out process is one of trial and error, at what point is it
advisable to stop so that the salaries generated by the structure are
competitive and at the same time payroll dollars are not used ineffectively or
irresponsibly?

Step 9: Review Differences Between Midpoints and Market Averages

The key to this step is to identify any large differences between proposed
midpoints and individual job-market averages. (See Table 7 on page 34.)

Key issue: The company must determine the percentage factor that should be
used to smooth out the midpoints.

Key questions to ask: Which jobs have the greater need to be competitively
paid? Can any jobs be underpaid without affecting the company's ability to
attract and retain employees? Can the company afford to overpay some jobs?

Step 10: Resolve Inconsistencies Between Internal and External Equity

The proposed salary structure shows how each of the evaluated positions
relates to one another internally as well as how each job relates to the market.
Most companies are comfortable if the proposed midpoints are within

GRADE	POINT SPREAD	POSITION	POINTS	MARKET AVERAGE	PROPOSED MIDPOINT	COMPA-RATIO	$\left(\dfrac{\text{PROPOSED MIDPOINT}}{\text{MARKET AVERAGE}}\right)$
TABLE 7							
11	527 +	Accounting Systems Control Officer Claims Officer Employee Relations Officer	550 565 545	$53,000 $57,000 $49,000	$53,000		100% 93% 108%
10	488-526	Open	—		$46,807		—
9	449-487	Team Leader	470	$36,000	$41,338		115%
8	410-448	Senior Accounting Consultant	425	$31,600	$36,509		116%
7	371-409	Project Coordinator	405	$29,200	$32,243		110%
6	332-370	Reconciliation Technician Records Management Specialist Accounting Consultant Accounting Technician	335 345 355 355	$23,000 $23,000 $24,300 $25,600	$28,476		124% 124% 117% 111%
5	293-331	Open	—		$25,149		—
4	254-292	Service Center Coordinator	260	$20,300	$22,211		109%
3	215-253	Open		—	$19,616		—
2	176-214	Copy Center Worker	210	$18,000	$17,324		96%
1	137-175	Mail Clerk	140	$15,300	$15,300		100%

10 percent of the competitive market. Using this as a rule of thumb, the following positions are most out of line with the market:

- Reconciliation Technician: 24 percent
- Records Management Specialist: 24 percent
- Accounting Consultant: 17 percent

With these proposed midpoints, the company will pay above the going rate in the market. If internal equity is a greater concern, then the additional money spent may not be a significant issue. However, another possibility to consider is pulling these jobs out of the proposed pay structure and paying them separately. The grade level would stay the same to provide internal job level equity, but the pay midpoints would represent the market more closely.

Decisions of this nature must be made after reviewing the inconsistencies. Each company must take into account its corporate culture and ability to pay when deciding what adjustments to make in the balance between internal values and external competitiveness. The key goal, as always, is to develop an acceptable pay structure that will aid the company in attracting, retaining and motivating qualified employees.

Key issue: Determining what is more important — internal or external equity.

Key questions to ask: What is the company culture? What is its stance on the consistent treatment of its employees? Is there high turnover in the company? Is it in a low-level job family or a high-level job family?

4

Pitfalls and Precautions

A pay structure is not an end in itself. In fact, it is possible for a company to pay its employees without having a formal pay structure. While pay structures help create a systematic and equitable system of cash-compensation management, it is important to keep in mind that they are only tools. Pay structures actually will burden a company unless the following issues are considered:

- Competitive posture. What is the competitive posture of the company? How much above or below the market should the company pay or can it afford to pay?

- Decision-making. Who will make the critical decisions underlying the pay structure? (For most companies, senior management tends to make these decisions.)

- Monitoring. How frequently will the pay structure be monitored and assessed for currency and appropriateness?

- Flexibility. Is the pay structure flexible enough to handle dynamic situations? This is critical in this age of constant change in corporations and in the economic environment, particularly the labor market.

- Resources. Can the company afford to allocate sufficient resources (including technology) to build and maintain current and relevant pay structures related to data?

- Communication. Is the company willing to allocate the required effort and resources to communicate the pay structures to employees and educate management in the proper use of pay structures?

Many companies currently are considering the "broadbanding" of salary ranges where applicable and appropriate. Broadbanding is the combining of existing ranges by expanding range width and reducing the number of grades. This usually is done for many reasons to benefit the organization and its employees. These reasons include the following:

- Paying for performance and allowing managers greater flexibility in salary administration

- Ease of moving people within the company

- Reduction of the demands of job evaluation as well as the time and effort required to make organizational changes.

Broadbanding is only one approach to pay administration in general and pay structures in particular.

Pay structures should be developed from the organization's mission and business strategy. Strategy should always precede structure development. Many internal and external environmental factors determine a company's pay structure. The pay structure has to adopt the same positive characteristics of a company's overall compensation program.

While designing a pay structure, a balance between internal and external equity must be maintained. Constant fine-tuning should take place. Developing pay structures is more an art than a science, although many mathematical techniques and processes may be used. While it is important to be specific about structural features such as the range spread, midpoint progression and so on, the key element of an effective pay structure is its value in functioning as a tool for managing pay.

$$\text{Midpoint} = \frac{(\text{Maximum} + \text{Minimum})}{2}$$

$$\text{Compa-Ratio} = \frac{\text{Base Salary}}{\text{Midpoint}} \quad \text{or} \quad \frac{\text{Company Midpoint}}{\text{Market Salary Average}}$$

$$\text{Spread on Either Side of the Midpoint} = \frac{\text{Midpoint} - \text{Minimum}}{\text{Midpoint}} \quad \text{[expressed as a negative percentage}\}$$

$$\frac{\text{Midpoint} - \text{Minimum}}{\text{Midpoint}} \quad \text{[expressed as a postive percentage}\}$$

$$\text{Range Spread} = \frac{(\text{Maximum} - \text{Minimum})}{\text{Minimum}}$$

$$\text{Maximum} = \text{Minimum} \times (1 + \text{Range Spread}) \qquad \text{Minimum} = \frac{\text{Maximum}}{(1 + \text{Range Spread})}$$

Midpoint Progression Matrix

In the case where midpoint progressions are to be calculated repeatedly over the long run, it is possible to develop a matrix for ready reference purposes. One such matrix is shown below. This matrix was developed using the "present value-future value formula, which is discussed on page 17 of this booklet. The vertical axis represents present value (PV), the horizontal axis represents future values (FV) and the number of grades used is eight (the number of intervals between grades, "n," is 7). The percentages listed are "i" values, where "i" is the percentage difference between midpoints.

For example, consider a present value of $10,000 and a future value of $50,000. The matrix shows that the constant difference between midpoints would be 25.85 percent. Remembering that $10,000 represents the midpoint of the lowest pay grade and $50,000 represents the midpoint of the highest pay grade, midpoints for all eight grades can be assigned by spacing them apart by 25.85 percent.

If the number of grades changes, a new matrix can be constructed using a different value or "n." Matrices can be developed quickly using a business calculator or computer.

$$PV = \frac{FV}{(1 + i)^n}$$

Highest Midpoint (FV)

	$50,000	$55,000	$60,000	$65,000	$70,000	$75,000	$80,000	$85,000	$90,000	$95,000	$100,000
$10,000	25.85%	27.58%	29.17%	30.66%	32.05%	33.35%	34.59%	35.76%	36.87%	37.94%	38.95%
$10,500	24.98%	26.69%	28.27%	29.75%	31.13%	32.43%	33.66%	34.82%	35.92%	36.98%	37.98%
$11,000	24.15%	25.85%	27.42%	28.89%	30.26%	31.55%	32.77%	33.92%	35.02%	36.07%	37.07%
$11,500	23.36%	25.05%	26.62%	28.07%	29.44%	30.72%	31.93%	33.08%	34.17%	35.21%	36.20%
$12,000	22.61%	24.30%	25.85%	27.30%	28.65%	29.93%	31.13%	32.27%	33.35%	34.39%	35.38%
$12,500	21.90%	23.57%	25.12%	26.56%	27.90%	29.17%	30.37%	31.50%	32.58%	33.61%	34.59%
$13,000	21.22%	22.88%	24.42%	25.85%	27.19%	28.45%	29.64%	30.77%	31.84%	32.86%	33.84%
$13,500	20.57%	22.22%	23.75%	25.17%	26.51%	27.76%	28.94%	30.06%	31.13%	32.15%	33.12%
$14,000	19.94%	21.59%	23.11%	24.52%	25.85%	27.10%	28.27%	29.39%	30.45%	31.46%	32.43%
$14,500	19.34%	20.98%	22.49%	23.90%	25.22%	26.46%	27.63%	28.74%	29.80%	30.80%	31.77%
$15,000	18.77%	20.40%	21.90%	23.30%	24.62%	25.85%	27.02%	28.12%	29.17%	30.17%	31.13%
$15,500	18.21%	19.83%	21.33%	22.73%	24.03%	25.26%	26.42%	27.52%	28.57%	29.56%	30.52%
$16,000	17.68%	19.29%	20.78%	22.17%	23.47%	24.69%	25.85%	26.94%	27.99%	28.98%	29.93%
$16,500	17.16%	18.77%	20.25%	21.64%	22.93%	24.15%	25.30%	26.39%	27.42%	28.41%	29.36%
$17,000	16.66%	18.26%	19.74%	21.12%	22.41%	23.62%	24.76%	25.85%	26.88%	27.87%	28.81%
$17,500	16.18%	17.77%	19.25%	20.62%	21.90%	23.11%	24.25%	25.33%	26.36%	27.34%	28.27%
$18,000	15.71%	17.30%	18.77%	20.13%	21.41%	22.61%	23.75%	24.83%	25.85%	26.83%	27.76%
$18,500	15.26%	16.84%	18.30%	19.66%	20.94%	22.14%	23.27%	24.34%	25.36%	26.33%	27.26%
$19,000	14.82%	16.40%	17.85%	19.21%	20.48%	21.67%	22.80%	23.87%	24.88%	25.85%	26.78%
$19,500	14.40%	15.97%	17.42%	18.77%	20.03%	21.22%	22.34%	23.41%	24.42%	25.38%	26.31%
$20,000	13.99%	15.55%	16.99%	18.34%	19.60%	20.78%	21.90%	22.96%	23.97%	24.93%	25.85%

Lowest Midpoint (PV) (vertical axis label)